THE SOUTH SUDAN I WANT

Seeing the Unseen

STEPHEN MATHIANG

A Note from the Publisher

The publisher wishes to acknowledge and thank Dr Douglas H. Johnson for his invaluable help and support for Africa World Books and its mission of preserving and promoting African cultural and literary traditions and history. Dr Johnson and fellow historians have been instrumental in ensuring that African people remain connected to their past and their identity. Africa World Books is proud to carry on this mission.

© Stephen Mathiang, 2015

ISBN: 978-0-6453010-8-3

Cover design, typesetting and layout : Africa World Books

Table of Contents

Dedication

This book is dedicated to all the South Sudanese, the current and future generations, the undeniable patriots.

Acknowledgements

I am indebted to my diligent editor, Wilson N. Macharia, and my very creative designer, Mary Maganga. These two made the book highly readable and attractive to behold.

For heaven's sake, I can't end there without expressing my sincere thanks to my dear wife, Elizabeth Agot Leek, and our beloved children, Ajoh, Kuch, Alier, Jogaak and Areu as well as my nephew, Kuch Bech Kuch. You have been prodding me on in life, so may the Lord bring people into your life to encourage you, too.

Preface

~~~

Most of this world's visionaries see the sky as the limit in the pursuit of their life's goals. But what they fail to understand is that the sky is too broad and too vast for anyone to make it a point of reference. In addition, the sky can be deceiving in that it begins as nearer as an inch above your head and spans beyond where your eye can see.

To avoid the unreasonableness of setting one's goal with the sky as the limit, some wiser visionaries set their eyes, not on the stars, but on a particular star. And though they may never reach it, that way they may at least have something to guide them towards greater human development and excellence.

My fellow South Sudanese too do not regard the moon or the sky as their limit, but they have chosen a particular star to be their national goal. Though they seem to miss the road towards that star temporarily due to some passing dark clouds, they are fully aware of what they are focusing on: Venus, the Morning Star. And the poems contained in this small book are intended to remind our people to keep focusing their eyes, their minds and their hearts on our life-long national guide, the Morning Star.

Intentionally, I beg to deviate from the normal way of writing poems for two primary reasons: first, I wish to make my message simple and straightforward for all the people to get; and, second, I want it to meet the requirements of our policymakers, especially those in the Ministry of Education, Science and Technology, so that they can make the book a class reader in both primary and secondary schools. This will make our children aware of our nation's vision at an early age and enable them to embrace and cherish poetry and, hopefully, trigger in them the desire to become national and global poets.

Introduction

The purpose of this poetic work is to evoke in our minds and those of others the kind of South Sudan we expect to have upon reaching Venus, our guiding star. As we press on to reconstruct and develop our young nation, we should do so with the end in mind. The resulting sharp vision will be inspiring enough to motivate us to surmount any difficulties that we may encounter as we march along the rough, meandering and thorny path that leads towards our goal. Foes, friends and brothers may stab us on the back to derail our plan of reaching the Morning Star, but we need to view at such as mere distractions and continue to march single-mindedly towards the goal. Achievers are always overcomers.

In this work, I target a few areas of our nation which, I believe, if given the attention they deserve can become reliable national pillars to build upon. I hope and wish you enjoy yielding yourself to the poetic spirit and fly places as you focus on the Morning Star, the Venus. And the South Sudan that we aspire for will unfold before your inner eyes.

My God-given Home

What a joy to have my own home, even if others despise it!

I have the potential to make my homeland better than others'!

The South Sudan I want is a nation that is landlocked;

It's the nation that shares her border with Ethiopia to the east;

It's the nation that shares her border with Kenya to the south-east;

It's the nation that shares her border with Uganda to the south;

It's the nation that shares her border with Congo (DRC) to the south-west;

It's the nation that shares her border with Central African Republic to the west;

It's the nation that shares her border with Sudan to the north;

It's the nation of whirring wings along the rivers of Cush;

It's the nation whose envoys sail in papyrus boats over many waters;

It's the nation divided by the longest river in the world;

It's the nation crisscrossed by numerous streams;

It's the home of tall, dark and smooth-skinned people;

It's the nation that has weathered many wars;

It's the nation whose people are feared far and wide due to their loyalty to their homeland;

It's the aggressive nation of strange speech because her citizens weathered tremendous hardships and emerged victorious;

This is the South Sudan I want, the nation I love and cherish;

This is my natural home;

I am proud to be South Sudanese;

It's my duty to make my nation great and respectable.

My home is my home, and yours is your home!

I love my home more than someone else's home!

The South Sudan I want is an integrated, united homeland;

It's the nation that is happy with herself;

It's the nation that doesn't permit others to violate her territorial integrity;

It's the nation that doesn't envy her neighbours;

It's the nation whose citizens see it as their life and blood;

It's the nation with abundant natural resources;

It's the nation of savanna and tropical forests;

It's the nation full of beautiful domestic animals and eye-catching wildlife;

It's the nation where the Nile and its tributaries meet to bless and sustain life;

It's the nation of sufficient annual rainfall, quenching the parched ground;

It's the nation that isn't highly populated, but boasts tracts of virgin land;

It's the nation that was once cursed but later repented and was forgiven by the Most High;

It's the nation whose citizens bring gifts to Mount Zion, the place of the Name of the Lord Almighty.

Stephen Mathiang

This is the South Sudan I want, the nation I love and cherish;
This is my natural home;
I am proud to be South Sudanese;
It's my duty to make my nation great and respectable.

"Whenever you can act, act as a liberator."
—Cyrus The Great

————o○o————

A Sovereign Nation

What a joy to be a part of free people in a free nation!

It takes sweat and blood to earn one's freedom, but it equally demands sacrifice through sweat and blood to maintain and protect it!

If you forfeit your hard-earned freedom, it will need more of your sweat and blood to regain it!

If you place less value on your freedom, it is because you don't know what it costs!

The South Sudan I want is a nation whose citizens are masters of their own destiny;

It's the nation whose citizens own, manage and steer their government along the most strategic path of development;

It's the nation whose government is the servant of the people, serving their needs holistically;

Stephen Mathiang | 17

It's the nation whose citizens know their past, present and future;

It's the nation whose citizens know when and how to lead and follow each other peacefully;

It's the nation where politics isn't a national curse but a respected exercise and a blessing;

It's the nation whose leaders aren't proud lords but just humble people's servants;

It's the nation whose citizens loyally serve their government, and their government in turn serves them sacrificially;

It's the nation whose citizens easily learn from their mistakes and strive not to repeat them or make new ones;

It's the nation whose citizens see and avoid thorns and snares on the path to national development;

It's the nation which isn't despised but greatly envied by the Queen of Sheba;

It's the nation of whirring wings along the rivers of Cush;

It's the nation whose envoys sail in papyrus boats over many waters;

This is the nation crisscrossed by rivers, the home of the Nile;

This is the nation whose people are feared far and wide because:

Their minds overflow with wisdom, knowledge and understanding, and

Their hearts are weighed down by love and compassion.

This is the aggressive nation of strange speech whose citizens embrace, cherish and uphold ethics for good governance.

It's the nation that was once cursed but repented and was forgiven by the Most High;

It's the nation whose citizens bring gifts to Mount Zion, the place of the Name of the Lord Almighty.

This is the South Sudan I want, the nation I love and cherish;

This is my natural home;

I am proud to be South Sudanese;

It's my duty to make my nation great and respectable.

"Many things have fallen, only to rise higher."
—Seneca

———OOO———

Stable Financial System

It is better to live within your means than to try to meet your excessive desires with other people's means;

It's noble to manage well the little you have before you start asking for more to manage;

The South Sudan I want is a nation whose financial system lies squarely on a solid rock;

It's a nation with stable financial system, with reliable, independent, professional people at the helm;

It's the nation where financial experts consistently monitor what comes in and what goes out;

It's the nation whose financial system is based on formidable pillars of checks and balances;

It's the nation whose financial system is in the hands of people with good moral values;

It's the nation whose taxpayers are happy to keep paying their dues for the good of their nation;

It's the nation where the nationals and foreigners compete to invest because of attractive returns;

It's the nation where local businesspeople move freely and with ease from nowhere to somewhere;

It's the nation with a strong economy and whose currency is not vulnerable to fluctuations;

It's the nation whose economists and financial professionals have the skills necessary to participate in the global market;

It's the nation whose National Anti-corruption Commission staff are well remunerated but have little work to do, for her citizens swim in the river of honesty;

It's the nation in which the IMF and the World Bank consistently invest without the need to police the national financial system;

It's the nation whose government undertake huge projects with little or no external support;

It's the nation whose citizens store up for themselves treasures where moth and rust don't destroy, and where thieves don't break in and steal;

It's the nation of whirring wings along the rivers of Cush;

Stephen Mathiang | 21

It's the nation whose envoys sail in papyrus boats over many waters;

This the nation divided by rivers, the home of the Nile;

This is the nation of tall, dark and smooth-skinned people;

It's the nation whose citizens are feared far and wide because of their reliable financial system;

It's the aggressive nation of strange speech because of her incredible financial system;

It's the nation that was once cursed but repented and was forgiven by the Most High;

It's the nation whose citizens bring gifts to Mount Zion, the place of the Name of the Lord Almighty.

This is the South Sudan I want, the nation I love and cherish;

This is my natural home;

I am proud to be South Sudanese;

It's my duty to make my nation great and respectable.

"Only when it is dark enough,
can you see the stars..."
—Ralph Waldo Emerson

———○○○———

The Values We Cherish

❧

The values you cherish define who you are!

If you like committing adultery, it is because you value promiscuity!

If you like stealing, it is because you value theft!

What you value and fill your mind with is portrayed in what you say or do.

The South Sudan I want is a nation that cherishes ethical values.

It's the nation where the lie is destroyed by the truth, and dishonesty is eliminated by honesty;

It's the nation where theft is a crime, and murder is duly punished by God and man;

It's the nation where immorality and other moral vices are drastically reduced;

Stephen Mathiang

It's the nation where people love the Lord with their entire being, and love each other as they love themselves;

It's the nation where men and women are seen as equal in the eyes of their Creator;

It's the nation where young people are cherished and nurtured with love by the adults;

It's the nation where old age is honoured, esteemed and cared for;

It's the nation where oppression and exploitation of man by man is viewed as an abomination;

It's the nation where people laugh with those who laugh and cry with those who cry;

It's the nation where human life is more precious than gold and diamond or cows, being regarded as sacred;

It's the nation where foreigners feel at home, enjoying the same level of respect as the locals;

It's the nation where ill-gotten gains are abhorred, but honest gains are approved of and their acquisition encouraged;

It's the nation where people are satisfied with what is theirs and respect what belongs to others;

It's the nation where moral behavior is viewed as more valuable than precious stone;

It's the nation where people equally and equitably share their national cake;

It's the nation where people bless their needy countrymen and others with their resources;

It's the nation where people speak to bless others but not to harm;

It's the nation where people lead to serve and bless their followers;

It's the nation where people follow to serve and uplift their leaders;

It's the nation without traitors but only loyalists and patriots;

It's the nation whose citizens embrace and defend what is morally right and shun what is ethically wrong;

It's the nation whose citizens jealously guard their nation without being provocative;

It's the nation where other creatures are not needlessly afraid of man, as they are properly managed and cared for in line with God's will;

It's the nation where justice flows like the Nile and righteousness like an ever-flowing river;

Stephen Mathiang | 25

It's the nation of whirring wings along the rivers of Cush;

It's the nation whose envoys sail in papyrus boats over many waters.

This is the nation crisscrossed by rivers, the home of the Nile;

This is the nation of tall, dark and smooth-skinned people;

It's the nation where citizens are feared far and wide for their refined manners;

It's the aggressive nation of strange speech known for her unbelievable ethical norms;

It's the nation that was once cursed but repented and was forgiven by the Most High;

It's the nation whose citizens bring gifts to Mount Zion, the place of the Name of the Lord Almighty.

This is the South Sudan I want, the nation I love and cherish;

This is my natural home;

I am proud to be South Sudanese;

It's my duty to make my nation great and respectable.

"Love the Lord your God with all your heart and with all your soul and with all your mind...and love your neighbor as yourself" (Matt.37-39).

———ooo———

Good Infrastructure

~~✦~~

Show me good infrastructure, and I will show you a good, strong nation!

A nation without good infrastructure is a nation with bleak future!

I better begin with the establishment of a reliable national infrastructure than waste huge resources on unsustainable projects; I should specialize in doing first thing first in life.

The South Sudan I want is a nation with excellent infrastructure.

It's the nation where road users don't envy those who fly;

It's the nation where those who sail do not envy road users or those who fly;

It's the nation where those who go by rail enjoy as much as road users and those who sail;

It's the nation where vehicles enjoy the road and last longer and longer;

It's the nation where motorcycles and bicycles admire the road and live long, too;

It's the nation where the vehicles, motorbikes and bicycles cross the Nile and its tributaries with ease;

It's the nation where beautiful motorboats and other vessels joyfully sail up and down the Nile and its tributaries;

It's the nation where artificial birds take off and land more gently and smoothly than real birds;

It's the nation where trains move meanderingly and smoothly across the land;

It's the nation where majestic skyscrapers scrape the beautiful sky;

It's the nation whose economy is founded upon thriving industries;

It's the nation with permanent academic, health and military institutions;

It's the nation with excellent water and sewage disposal systems;

It's the nation whose power grid extends to the remotest village;

It's the nation where nothing is left to chance, a haven of great thinkers and artists;

It's the nation with broad-range, wide-coverage infrastructure;

It's the nation of whirring wings along the rivers of Cush;

It's the nation whose envoys sail in papyrus boats over many waters.

This the nation crisscrossed by rivers, the home of the Nile;

This is the nation of tall, dark and smooth-skinned people;

It's the nation whose citizens are feared far and wide for the excellent infrastructure of their nation;

It's the aggressive nation of strange speech known for her high level of infrastructure;

It's the nation once cursed but repented and was forgiven by the Most High;

It's the nation whose citizens bring gifts to Mount Zion, the place of the Name of the Lord Almighty.

This is the South Sudan I want, the nation I love and cherish;

This is my natural home;

I am proud to be South Sudanese;

It's my duty to make my nation great and respectable.

Therefore everyone who hears these words of mine and puts them into practice is like a wise man who builds his house on the rock. The rain came down, the streams rose, and the winds blew and beat against that house; yet it did not fall, because it had its foundation on the rock. But everyone who hears these words of mine and does not put them into practice is like a foolish man who built his house on sand. The rain came down, the streams rose, and the winds blew and beat against that house, and it fell with a great crash (Matt.7:24-27).

———OOO———

Stephen Mathiang | 31

High Spirit of
Nationalism

~sju~

There are people who are neither tribalists nor nationalists but just themselves, merely adoring their egocentric lives; give such a nation of their own, and they let it down!

They are happy as long as their selfish desires are satisfied, even if that happens at the expense of others;

Glorify God in your life, and I just call you nothing but a child of God;

Glorify self in your life, and I just call you nothing but selfish;

Glorify your tribe in your life, and I just call you nothing but a tribalist;

Glorify your nation in your life, and I just call you nothing but a nationalist;

Just show me where you place your nation in your life, and I will tell you who you are.

Blessed is the nation whose citizens are patriots, with the spirit of nationalism streaming high in their blood;

Like arrows in the hands of a warrior are patriots who safeguard their nation;

Blessed is the nation whose quiver is full of them, for they won't be put to shame when they contend with their enemies at their national gates.

The South Sudan I want is a nation where tribalism has been swallowed up by nationalism.

It's the nation where nationalism is the umbrella that shelters the different tribes from harsh weather of ethnic conflict;

It's the nation where patriotism is in the bloodstream of her citizens;

It's the nation whose citizens regard themselves as brothers and sisters despite their diverse ethnic backgrounds, geographical location, creed, economic status or political affiliation;

It's the nation whose citizens aren't judged by the language they speak but by their conduct;

Stephen Mathiang | 33

It's the nation in which any citizen can live and work peacefully within her borders;

It's the nation whose citizens freely intermarry to beautifully colour the national blood;

It's the nation whose citizens view their unique tribes as beautiful, harmless national colours;

It's the nation whose citizens regard their country with pride;

It's the nation of whirring wings along the rivers of Cush;

It's the nation whose envoys sail in papyrus boats over many waters;

It's the nation crisscrossed by rivers, the home of the Nile;

It's the nation of tall, dark and smooth-skinned people;

It's the nation whose citizens are feared far and wide for their admirable spirit of patriotism;

It's the aggressive nation of strange speech where diverse tribes unite rather than divide;

It's the nation that was once cursed but repented and was forgiven by the Most High;

It's the nation whose citizens bring gifts to Mount Zion, the place of the Name of the Lord Almighty.

This is the South Sudan I want, the nation I love and cherish;

This is my natural home;

I am proud to be South Sudanese;

It's my duty to make my nation great and respectable.

How good and pleasant it is when brothers live together in unity! It is like precious oil poured on the head, running down on the beard, running down on Aaron's beard, down upon the collar of his robes. It is as if the dew of Hermon were falling on Mount Zion. For there the Lord bestows his blessing, even life forevermore (Ps.133).

———ooo———

Stephen Mathiang | 35

Innovative Education

꧁꧂

Teach the heart through the mind, and you have an innovative education!

Teach the mind without reaching the heart, and you have a destructive education!

The South Sudan I want is a nation with highly educated, yet humble people;

It's the nation whose citizens learn and civilize, not to destroy but to build;

It's the nation where education betters human life and improves natural environment;

It's the nation where educational papers speak less but act a lot;

It's the nation where educational papers aren't people but mere tools in the hands of man;

It's the nation where illiteracy has been buried once for all;

It's the nation where ignorance is buried alive;

It's the nation of whirring wings along the rivers of Cush;

It's the nation whose envoys sail in papyrus boats over many waters.

This is the nation divided by rivers, the home of the Nile;

This is the nation of tall, dark and smooth-skinned people.

This is the South Sudan I want, the nation I love and cherish;

This is my natural home;

I am proud to be South Sudanese;

It's my duty to make my nation great and respectable.

If my education negatively impacts my life, my family, my community, my nation and my world, then I am unschooled!

But if my education brings positive changes to my life, my family, my community, my nation and my world, then I have something to be proud of, making others to be proud, too!

The South Sudan I want is the one whose education contributes to world civilization;

It's the nation where education leads to important discoveries in life;

It's the nation where education appreciates and promotes entrepreneurial spirit;

Stephen Mathiang | 37

It's the nation whose citizens create jobs for themselves and for others;

It's the nation of minimal unemployment;

It's the nation where teaching post is favorable and highly esteemed;

It's the nation where children aren't left to face the walls while teachers scramble for their meal;

It's the nation of first things first;

It's the nation whose citizens are feared far and wide for being highly educated;

It's the aggressive nation of strange speech due to her technical innovation;

It's the nation that was once cursed but repented and was forgiven by the Most High;

It's the nation whose citizens bring gifts to Mount Zion, the place of the Name of the Lord Almighty.

This is the South Sudan I want, the nation I love and cherish;

This is my natural home;

I am proud to be South Sudanese;

It's my duty to make my nation great and respectable.

"Education is the great engine of personal development. It is through education that the daughter of a peasant can become a doctor, that a son of a mineworker can become the head of the mine, that a child of farm workers can become the president of a nation."
—Nelson Mandela

———○○○———

High Standard of Living

W ho wants to live a poor life under the sun?

A poor man is always despised by others, including his own kinsmen;

The power, authority and wisdom lie, not with the poor but with the rich, even if they are obvious traits of the poor and not of the rich.

What a privilege for one to enjoy God's gifts under the sun!

What a privilege for one to realize his full potential while on earth for his own benefit!

What a privilege for one to bless the needy with his honestly acquired resources!

What a joy to be a giver rather than to be a receiver in life, unless fate demands otherwise!

It's a blessing for one to enjoy life under the sun before he goes on a journey of no return!

Nationalists anywhere aren't politically free unless they are also socially and economically free!

The South Sudan I want is a nation whose citizens enjoy a high standard of living;

It's the nation whose citizens are as busy as bees and ants;

It's the nation whose citizens cherish and promote self-esteem;

It's the nation whose citizens cherish and encourage self-sufficiency;

It's the nation whose citizens refuse handouts but sweat to live proudly;

It's the nation whose citizens abhor short-cuts to life but derive joy from doing things the right way;

It's the nation whose citizens diligently exploit natural resources to enrich themselves and others;

It's the nation whose citizens make good use of the gifts that God has given them;

It's the nation of whirring wings along the rivers of Cush;

It's the nation whose envoys sail in papyrus boats over many waters.

Stephen Mathiang

This the nation crisscrossed by rivers, the home of the Nile;

This is the nation of tall, dark and smooth-skinned people;

It's the nation whose citizens are feared far and wide for their high standard of living;

It's the aggressive nation of strange speech due to the comfortable life of her citizens.

This is the South Sudan I want, the nation I love and cherish;

This is my natural home;

I am proud to be South Sudanese;

It's my duty to make my nation great and respectable.

There is always joy and dignity when one lives on the outcomes of his toil!

For Apostle Paul commands us not to eat unless we work;

For the wise man admonishes us with these words based on Prov. 24:30-34:

I went past the field of the sluggard, past the vineyard of the man who lacks judgement; thorns had come up everywhere, the ground was covered with weeds, and the stone wall was in ruins. I applied my heart to what I observed and learned a lesson from what I saw: A little sleep, a little slumber, a little folding of the hands to rest – and poverty will come on you like a bandit and scarcity like an armed man.

Hence, the South Sudan I want is a nation where idleness is swallowed up by hard work.

It's the nation where fraudulent way of life is viewed as an abomination and a crime;

It's the nation where land and waters and all things therein are meant to benefit man;

It's the nation where atmospheric benefits benefit people;

It's the nation where the rich don't use the poor as a ladder to acquire more wealth;

It's the nation where the gap between the rich and the poor is negligible;

It's the nation where the entire citizenry live well above the internationally acknowledged poverty line;

It's the nation where children inherit wealth to maintain and grow it further;

It's the nation where the citizens have enough to live on and extra to bless others with;

Stephen Mathiang | 43

It's the nation where aliens join hands with the nationals to invest and expand the economy further;

It's the nation that was once cursed but repented and was forgiven by the Most High;

It's the nation whose citizens bring gifts to Mount Zion, the place of the Name of the Lord Almighty.

This is the South Sudan I want, the nation I love and cherish;

This is my natural home;

I am proud to be South Sudanese;

It's my duty to make my nation great and respectable.

"Start by doing what's necessary;
then do what's possible; and suddenly
you are doing the impossible."
—Francis of Assisi

———oOo———

Excellent Healthcare

⚬⚬⚬

Healthy people make the nation healthy, socially, politically and economically!

It breaks God's heart to see his creatures dangling in the merciless jaws of disease!

The South Sudan I want is a nation whose people enjoy quality but affordable healthcare;

It's the nation that intentionally invests heavily in healthcare;

It's the nation where health workers are people-centered, compassionate and God-fearing;

It's the nation where physicians don't think they know but know they know;

It's the nation where physicians don't treat to kill but to cure, unless nature demands the right of the way;

It's the nation where public hospitals offer better services than private ones;

It's the nation where scientific and technological innovations and discoveries enhance healthcare;

Stephen Mathiang | 45

It's the nation where the environment is friendly and healthy;

It's the nation where health experts aggressively promote national healthcare;

It's the nation where healthcare experts fully participate in the promotion of the global healthcare;

It's the nation where healthcare workers are highly motivated to love and excel in their work;

It's the nation where foreigners seek and enjoy health benefits;

It's the nation of whirring wings along the rivers of Cush;

It's the nation whose envoys sail in papyrus boats over many waters.

This is the nation crisscrossed by rivers, the home of the Nile;

This is the nation of tall, dark and smooth-skinned people;

It's the nation whose citizens are feared far and wide for their advanced healthcare facilities.

It's the aggressive nation of strange speech, known for her excellent healthcare policies.

This is the South Sudan I want, the nation I love and cherish;

This is my natural home;

I am proud to be South Sudanese;

It's my duty to make my nation great and respectable.

If other nations have excellent healthcare, why can't my nation have one?

The South Sudan I want is a nation whose citizens see diseases, not as life-threatening but as controllable and manageable.

It's the nation whose citizens eat healthy food and drink healthy drinks;

It's the nation whose citizens don't envy foreign healthcare but love theirs;

It's the nation whose citizens see healthcare and health workers as their own;

It's the nation whose children are born to live and realize their life's goals;

It's the nation whose senior citizens aren't robbed of their sweet, last phase of life by disease;

It's the nation whose citizens' incomes aren't eaten up by disease;

It's the nation that was once cursed but repented and was forgiven by the Most High;

It's the nation whose citizens bring gifts to Mount Zion, the place of the Name of the Lord Almighty.

This is the South Sudan I want, the nation I love and cherish;

This is my natural home;

I am proud to be South Sudanese;

It's my duty to make my nation great and respectable.

"The Lord said to Moses, 'Make a snake and put it up on a pole; anyone who is bitten can look at it and live.' So Moses made a bronze snake and put it up on a pole. Then when anyone was bitten by a snake and looked at the bronze snake, he lived" (Num.21:8-9).

―――――○○○―――――

Respect for Humanity

God made man plain and simple, but man has made himself more complicated!

Though there are man-made problems facing mankind, man to man must remain a brother;

Though I turn another man to be my enemy, it won't remove my problems but increase them instead;

But if I make friendship with another man, he will help me handle my problems, and I too will help him handle his problems;

The world is full of problems because man has made himself to be his own enemy;

Man wastes his time and energy trying to control and rule over man;

But men should, instead, come together to rule over the fish of the sea and the birds of the air, over the livestock, over all the earth, and over all the creatures that move along the ground as decreed by their Creator.

Stephen Mathiang

The South Sudan I want is a nation in which the worst enemy of man isn't man himself.

It's the nation where the enemy isn't fellow man but hunger and poverty;

It's the nation where the enemy isn't fellow man but disease;

It's the nation where the foe isn't fellow man but illiteracy and ignorance;

It's the nation where the enemy isn't fellow man but poor moral values;

It's the nation where the foe isn't fellow man but insecurity;

It's the nation where the enemy isn't fellow man but natural disasters;

It's the nation where the foe isn't fellow man but poor infrastructure and backwardness;

It's the nation of whirring wings along the rivers of Cush;

It's the nation whose envoys sail in papyrus boats over many waters.

This the nation crisscrossed by rivers, the home of the Nile;

This is the nation of tall, dark and smooth-skinned people;

This is the nation whose citizens are feared far and wide for being humane;

This is the aggressive nation of strange speech whose citizens regard all human beings as brothers and sisters;

This is the South Sudan I want, the nation I love and cherish;

This is my natural home;

I am proud to be South Sudanese;

It's my duty to make my nation great and respectable.

Be humane before you expect others to be compassionate!

The rule of the thumb from above commands us to love others as we love ourselves;

Thus, the South Sudan I want is a nation where people love others as themselves;

It's the nation where love has swallowed up hatred;

It's the nation where humility has dethroned pride;

It's the nation where gender equality is embraced and promoted;

It's the nation where people see themselves as equal in the eyes of a compassionate God;

Stephen Mathiang | 51

It's the nation where people embrace and promote human dignity;

It's the nation where every man regards the other as a brother;

It's the nation where foreign visitors feel at home unless they are there to cause problems;

It's the nation where human rights are valued and protected;

It's the nation that was once cursed but repented and was forgiven by the Most High;

It's the nation whose citizens bring gifts to Mount Zion, the place of the Name of the Lord Almighty.

This is the South Sudan I want, the nation I love and cherish;

This is my natural home;

I am proud to be South Sudanese;

It's my duty to make my nation great and respectable.

"Do nothing out of selfish ambition or vain conceit, but in humility consider others better than yourselves. Each of you should look not only to your own interests, but also to the interests of others" (Phil.2:3-4).

———OOO———

Religious Freedom

Sacred issues belong to spiritual realm;
   Sacred matters are personal matters;
Sacred issues have to do with personal relationship between man and his God;
   Sacred issues are meant to make human life bearable and to lift it to the highest level of joy;
   Sacred issues aren't sacred any longer if they make human life miserable.

I am happy if my religious faith makes me and others happy!
I am happy if my religious faith makes my God happy!
   The South Sudan I want is a nation where God is the Lord;
   It's the nation where faith in God is individualized;
   It's the nation where people aren't victimized for the religion of their choice;

Stephen Mathiang

It's the nation where religion unites rather than divides people;

It's the nation where religion contributes to human development and prosperity;

It's the nation where religion is for the good of man, not for his destruction;

It's the nation where people of different faiths coexist peacefully;

It's the nation where destructive religious practices are frowned upon and reined in;

It's the nation where destructive and misleading religious teachings are shunned;

It's the nation whose citizens see themselves as human beings and God as God;

It's the nation whose people don't judge each other by creed but by conduct;

It's the nation whose citizens practise religion in a way that is right and acceptable worldwide;

It's the nation of whirring wings along the rivers of Cush;

It's the nation whose envoys sail in papyrus boats over many waters.

This is the nation crisscrossed by rivers, the home of the Nile;

This is the nation of tall, dark and smooth-skinned people;

It's the nation whose citizens are feared far and wide for their admirable religious practices;

It's the aggressive nation of strange speech, known for her high level of religious tolerance.

It's the nation that was once cursed but repented and was forgiven by the Most High;

It's the nation whose citizens bring gifts to Mount Zion, the place of the Name of the Lord Almighty.

This is the South Sudan I want, the nation I love and cherish;

This is my natural home;

I am proud to be South Sudanese;

It's my duty to make my nation great and respectable.

> *"We are never defeated unless*
> *we give up on God."*
> —Ronald Reagan

> *Have I not commanded you? Be strong*
> *and courageous. Do not be afraid; do not*
> *be discouraged, for the Lord your God*
> *will be with you wherever you go.*
> (Joshua 1:9).

Stephen Mathiang

I hate, I despise your religious feasts; I cannot stand your assemblies. Even though you bring me burnt offerings and grain offerings, I will not accept. Away with the noise of your songs! I will not listen to the music of your harps. But let justice roll on like a river, righteousness like a never-falling streams (Amos 5:21-24).

———○○○———

Stable Security

Many keys and padlocks plus barking dogs don't guarantee the security of my house!

Many keys and padlocks plus barking dogs don't guarantee the security of my nation!

A nation whose citizens and their possessions aren't secure within and without their homes is unsafe nation;

A nation where the strong takes advantage of the weak isn't safe at all;

If I provide my own security, I'm nothing but a stateless man;

The security of my life and my property is paramount, showing that I'm a secure citizen in a secure nation;

The security of my nation means the security of her citizens.

The South Sudan I want is a nation in which man and his possessions are completely safe.

It's the nation where national assets are valued and safeguarded by all;

It's the nation where the protection of man is the primary duty of the government;

It's the nation where the poor and the weak aren't the victims of the rich and strong;

It's the nation where man isn't trained and armed to kill fellow man but to protect him from external harm;

It's the nation where armed men do not turn their weapons on each other but see each other as comrades in arms;

It's the nation where the armed forces protect the people's government rather than seeking to bring it down;

It's the nation where man is trained and armed to protect his nation's boundaries;

It's the nation where the might of the tongue is more powerful and valued than the might of the sword;

It's the nation where people are safe to go by train, drive, fly and enjoy boat ride;

It's the nation where arrogance and pride are seen as enemies of security;

It's the nation where humility isn't regarded as a weakness but as strength and a sign of maturity;

It's the nation where law breakers aren't eliminated but quarantined so as to reform and be restored to society;

It's the nation where immoral people aren't left to disturb people's peace but quarantined to reform and rehabilitate;

It's the nation where man doesn't destroy but rules peacefully over the fish of the sea, the birds of the air and over every living creature that moves on the ground;

It's the nation of whirring wings along the rivers of Cush;

It's the nation whose envoys sail in papyrus boats over many waters.

This is the nation that is divided by rivers, the home of the Nile;

This is the nation of tall, dark and smooth-skinned people;

It's the nation whose citizens are feared far and wide for the level of security they enjoy;

It's the aggressive nation of strange speech, known for her high level of safety.

This is the South Sudan I want, the nation I love and cherish;

This is my natural home;

I am proud to be South Sudanese;

It's my duty to make my nation great and respectable.

I'm tired of my electrified, razor-wired fence that keeps me away from my brother!

Mankind must embrace and cherish peaceful co-existence;

The South Sudan I want is a nation that is safe for all living creatures.

It's the nation whose citizens aren't afraid of each other but love one another;

It's the nation whose citizens live in peace with foreigners;

It's the nation whose citizens don't fear the night or the day;

It's the nation whose citizens love to see their children going out in peace and coming back the same way;

It's the nation that was once cursed but repented and was forgiven by the Most High;

It's the nation whose citizens bring gifts to Mount Zion, the place of the Name of the Lord Almighty.

This is the South Sudan I want, the nation I love and cherish;

This is my natural home;

I am proud to be South Sudanese;

It's my duty to make my nation great and respectable.

The Lord is my Shepard, I shall not be in want. He makes me lie down in green pastures, he leads me beside quiet waters, he restores my soul. He guides me in paths of righteousness for his name's sake. Even though I walk through the valley of the shadow of death, I will fear no evil, for you are with me; your rod and your staff, they comfort me. You prepare a table before me in the presence of my enemies. You anoint my head with oil; my cup overflows. Surely goodness and love will follow me all the days of my life, and I will dwell in the house of the Lord forever (Ps.23).

———OOO———

Good Foreign Relations

If my relationship with you leads to your domination of me or my domination of you, then we aren't mutually related; we better reconsider or break it off.

If my relationship with you betters my life's situation and yours, then we are mutually related and we better maintain and improve on it;

Mine is one of many islands, but none of the other islands is mine or mine theirs;

These many islands, though, differ in terms of size, age, political and economic maturity;

These many islands desire and agree to mutually relate to each other in a friendly manner in spite of their significant differences;

As no man is superior or inferior to his fellow man, and since an island is nothing but the home of the free man, no island is superior or inferior to another island;

Far better if islands encourage one another, build each other up and carry each other's burdens in love, never becoming tired of doing what is right.

The South Sudan I want is a nation that enjoys harmonious relationship with all other countries.

It's the nation where diplomacy is meant for mutual benefits;

It's the nation whose diplomats exhibit deep sense of humanity and moral excellence in their work;

It's the nation whose diplomats act as strong, reliable bridges for connecting their nation with other nations;

It's the nation whose diplomats are known for expertise in their work;

It's the nation whose diplomats keep raising their skills for the benefit of their nation;

It's the nation whose diplomats render informed, objective advice to their people's government with the aim of making their nation effectively play her role in the international community;

It's the nation whose diplomats put national interest above their personal interests;

Stephen Mathiang | 63

It's the nation whose diplomats subject their words, deeds and thoughts to the test of national values;

It's the nation whose diplomats know how to market their nation abroad without flattering or slapping their nation's leaders on the back;

It's the nation whose diplomats avoid anything that may bring disrepute to their motherland;

It's the nation whose diplomats won't permit others to take unfair advantage of their people;

It's the nation whose diplomats diligently serve and safeguard their nationals in foreign lands;

It's the nation whose diplomats facilitate and coordinate trade between their nation and other countries;

It's the nation whose diplomats won't meddle in the private affairs of foreign nations but, instead, render objective advice, if need be;

It's the nation whose diplomats remarkably contribute to a healthy global diplomacy;

It's the nation of whirring wings along the rivers of Cush;

It's the nation whose envoys sail in papyrus boats over many waters.

This is the nation crisscrossed by rivers, the home of the Nile;

This is the nation of tall, dark and smooth-skinned people;

It's the nation whose citizens are feared far and wide for their admirable foreign policy;

It's the aggressive nation of strange speech that has excelled in handling her foreign relatios, despite her late addition to the community of nations;

It's the nation that was once cursed but repented and was forgiven by the Most High;

It's the nation whose citizens bring gifts to Mount Zion, the place of the Name of the Lord Almighty.

This is the South Sudan I want, the nation I love and cherish;

This is my natural home;

I am proud to be South Sudanese;

It's my duty to make my nation great and respectable.

"We are therefore Christ's ambassadors, as though God were making his appeal through us" (2Cor.5:20a).

―――――OOO―――――

What it Takes to Reach the Morning Star

~~❧~~

What a joy for a nation to have specific, measurable, achievable, realistic and time-bound plans to realize her vision!

What a joy for a nation to have people whose actions match their words as they move their nation towards her goal!

What a joy for a nation to have citizens who have the spirit of persistence and resilience to enable them realize the vision of their nation!

What a joy for South Sudan to be one of these farsighted nations under the sun!

In her case, reaching the Morning Star can be as simple as taking a walk in the cool of the day when good intentions are behind the walk. If not so, the endeavour can be as dangerous and scaring as hiking to the top of Mount Everest.

To reach the Morning Star, intensive awareness about the national mission to the

Venus should be carried out among the sons and daughters of South Sudan.

To reach the Morning Star, it behoves that the torch bearers be passionate and press ahead single-mindedly.

To reach the Morning Star, the change of the torch bearers, when necessary, should be done peacefully and agreeably.

To reach the Morning Star, all the sons and daughters of our beloved land should follow the torch bearers obediently and tirelessly.

To reach the Morning Star calls for the unity of hearts, minds and souls of both the leaders and followers.

To reach the Morning Star, any distraction, deviation from the course, dispute or fighting along the road towards realizing the national vision, should be avoided.

To reach the Morning Star, the marchers should be fully aware of and safeguard themselves from local and international 'road attackers and hijackers'.

To reach the Morning Star, the marchers should be well aware of their real, loyal supporters.

To reach the Morning Star, all national resources should be committed fully to this noble, and worthy mission.

To reach the Morning Star, the spirit of hatred, revenge, pride, selfishness, greed and divisiveness among the marchers should be shunned.

To reach the Morning Star, the spirit of unity, forgiveness, brotherhood, humility, honesty, selflessness, caring and understanding among the marchers should be embraced and sustained!

The nation that considers reaching the Morning Star as her vision is the Republic of South Sudan.

This is the nation of whirring wings along the rivers of Cush;

This is the nation whose envoys sail in papyrus boats over many waters;

This is the nation crisscrossed by rivers, the home of the Nile;

This is the nation of tall, dark and smooth-skinned people;

This is the nation whose citizens are feared far and wide for their admirable resolve to reach the Morning Star, the Venus;

Stephen Mathiang | 69

This is the aggressive nation of strange speech, which has well-thought-out plans to realize her vision, the Morning Star, despite her late birth in the global society;

This is the nation that was once cursed but repented and was forgiven by the Most High;

This is the nation whose citizens bring gifts to Mount Zion, the place of the Name of the Lord Almighty.

This is the South Sudan I want, the nation I love and cherish;

This is my natural home;

I am proud to be South Sudanese.

It's my duty to make my nation great and respectable.

Plans that are sure to succeed and benefit mankind belong to the Lord, for he says:

"For I know the plans I have for you,
plans to prosper you and not to harm you,
plans to give you hope and a future"
(Jer.29:11).

My Wishes

I wish my people would understand fully that obtaining a national independence is one thing, but maintaining and moving conscientiously the nation forward towards its set goal is quite another!

I wish my people would fully know that any tiresome trip to national vision doesn't need the participation of greedy, gluttonous, selfish people!

I wish my people would well know that any national vision is only realized by those who are accountable to their words, deeds and thoughts!

I wish my people would fully comprehend that the zigzagged journey to any national vision always requires solid unity of hearts, minds and souls of the trekkers!

I wish my people would take the bull by the horns and march single-mindedly to their national vision, the Venus!

Stephen Mathiang | 71

I wish my people would know very well that any national vision isn't reached always by half-hearted people!

I wish my people would fully understand that the road to the Venus has a lot of ups and downs, twists and turns!

I wish my people would fully understand that there isn't easy sail always to any national vision under the sun!

I wish my people would tighten their belts and march along the rough path to their Morning Star, the focal point of hope!

I wish my people would fully understand that those who seem to have reached their national vision had shed their tremendous sweats and bloods and expended other voluble resources to arrive there!

I wish my people would understand that the road to any nation's vision is always led by those who know the way, the visionary people!

I wish my people would fully comprehend that it is wise always to follow diligently those who know the way to national vision without derailing them along the road!

I wish my people would understand correctly that there is always wisdom and courage in giving way to those who know the way to national vision if you don't know the way very well!

I wish my people would clearly understand that it is always wise and honoring for your fellowmen to recognize that you know well the way to national vision, and then ask you to lead them, than you blowing your own trumpet and imposing yourself to lead them against their will!

I wish my people would appreciate the fact that it is humiliating to oneself and his family and equally embarrassing to God and man for a short-sighted person to insist on leading others towards the national vision and continue insisting on doing so until his followers and God disqualify him and push him aside!

I wish my people would know very well that people rarely arrived at their designated destination if they leave the mission and start quarrelling and fighting among themselves!

I wish my people would understand that avoiding injuring one another and forgiving each other along the path of national vision is the secret to the success of their mission!

I wish the gracious and loving God would touch the hearts of my people to forgive one another, reconcile their differences and march in one accord towards their national vision, the Morning Star or the Venus!

I wish my people would eventually arrive joyfully at their national destination, the Morning Star, for their own good and the general welfare of their children's children as well as for the glory of God!

Then I would be happy to say that this is the South Sudan I want!

This is the South Sudan I want, the nation I love and cherish!

This is the nation of whirring wings along the rivers of Cush;

This is the nation whose envoys sail in papyrus boats over many waters;

This is the nation crisscrossed by rivers, the home of the Nile;

This is the nation of tall, dark and smooth-skinned people;

This is the nation whose citizens are feared far and wide for their remarkable wisdom and unwavering determination;

This is the aggressive nation of strange speech that has arrived at her vision, the Morning Star, despite her late birth among global nations;

This is the nation that was once cursed but repented and was forgiven by the Most High;

This is the nation whose citizens bring gifts to Mount Zion, the place of the Name of the Lord Almighty.

This is the South Sudan I want, the nation I love and cherish;

This is my natural home;

I am proud to be South Sudanese;

It's my duty to make my nation great and respectable.

"Delight yourself in the Lord and he will give you the desires of your heart"
(Ps. 37:4).

———OOO———

Conclusion

The South Sudan I love and call home happens to be landlocked, yet endowed in many ways by God;

The South Sudan I want is a nation whose citizens are masters of their own fate;

The South Sudan I want is a nation whose financial system is founded on the solid rock of a thriving economy and shrewd financial managers;

The South Sudan I want is a nation founded on excellent ethical values;

The South Sudan I want is a nation with excellent infrastructure;

The South Sudan I want is a nation where tribalism is swallowed up by nationalism;

The South Sudan I want is a nation that is globally recognized for high quality education;

The South Sudan I want is a nation whose citizens enjoy a high standard of living;

The South Sudan I want is a nation known for quality, yet affordable healthcare;

The South Sudan I want is a nation in which the worst enemy of man isn't man himself;

The South Sudan I want is a nation where God is the Lord;

The South Sudan I want is a nation where man and his possessions are truly safe;

The South Sudan I want is a nation that enjoys harmonious relationship with other nations.

The South Sudan I want is a nation with specific, measurable, achievable, realistic and time-bound plans to attain her vision!

This is the nation of whirring wings along the rivers of Cush;

This is the nation whose envoys sail in papyrus boats over many waters;

This is the nation divided by rivers, the home of the Nile;

This is the nation of tall, dark and smooth-skinned people;

This is the nation whose citizens are feared far and wide for having realized their national vision, the Morning Star or Venus;

This is the aggressive nation of strange speech that chose the Morning Star as the emblem of her flag in spite of her late appearance on the global scene as a nation state;

This is the nation that was once cursed but repented and was forgiven by the Most High;

This is the nation whose citizens bring gifts to Mount Zion, the place of the Name of the Lord Almighty.

This is the South Sudan I want, the nation I love and cherish;

This is my natural home;

I am proud to be South Sudanese;

It's my duty to make my nation great and respectable.

It is unwise for me to sit back and criticize others for not working at making my nation great; instead, it is my national duty to share my own opinions through thoughts, words or deeds with my concerned fellow citizens to see how we can together build a better nation for ourselves and for our children's children.

Shunning the feeling of frustration and the spirit of blaming others and creating anarchy, I shall persistently proclaim what I believe is right before man and God with the hope that people will one day acknowledge or recall my viewpoint when the truth assumes the rule. And when they own and act on it, I will still be happy for having contributed to their welfare and the good of others.

Long live South Sudan!

Government of the people, by the people, for the people, shall not perish from the earth
—Abraham Lincoln

———ooo———

South Sudan–Sudan boundary represents
January 1, 1956 alignment; final alignment
pending negotiations and demarcation.

SUDAN

Abyei
region

indefinite

Raga

Aweil

Bentiu

Malakal

Warab

As
Sudd

Wau

Tonj

CENTRAL
AFRICAN
REPUBLIC

Rumbek

Bor

Boma

White Nile
(Bahr al Jabal)

JUBA

Yambio

Torit

Nimule

Ilemi
Triangle

Kinyeti

ETHIOPIA

DEMOCRATIC REPUBLIC
OF THE CONGO

Congo

KENYA

UGANDA

0   100 200 km
0   100   200 mi

SUDAN

National Capital
State Capital
Significant Town
International Boundary
State Boundary
Administrative Boundary
Paved Road
Fresh Water Marsh

January 1, 1956
Line of Demarcation